આ મારી ચોપડી છે!

(aa maaree chopaDee chhe!)

_____

_____

I love Gujarati

Gnaana Publishing
PO Box 10513
Fullerton, CA 92838
inspire@gnaana.com
www.gnaana.com

Text © 2016 Avni Gandhi
Illustrations © 2016 Ajanta Guhathakurta
Book design by Sara Petrous

With special thanks to Madhu Rye.

10 9 8 7 6 5 4 3 2 1

Cataloging-in-Publication Data available at the Library of Congress.

ISBN 978-1-943018-24-6 (Book)
ISBN 978-1-943018-25-3 (Book with Audio CD)

કાચબાનો ક

Ka Kaachbaano Ka

A Poetical Introduction
to the Gujarati Alphabet

Written by
AVNI GANDHI

Illustrations by
AJANTA GUHATHAKURTA

gnaana

કેમ છો?
(kem chho?)

મજામાં છો?
(majaamaaM chho?)

મારું નામ કવિ છે.
(maaruM naam kavi chhe.)

I love to make words rhyme.

ગુજરાતી શીખવા તૈયાર છો?

(gujaraatee sheekhvaa taiyaar chho?)

I'm sure we will have a good time!

Gujarati is a language that evolved from Sanskrit and is native to Gujarat, a state in the western part of India. It is spoken by over 65 million people across the world, including in Pakistan, Bangladesh, Fiji, Kenya, Uganda, Australia, New Zealand, Canada, the United States, and Panama! No matter where you go in the world, you will always to find a Gujarati *bhai* (brother) or *ben* (sister) who will be happy to hear you ask, "*Kem chho?*"

અ	આ	ઇ	ઈ	ઉ	ઊ	ઋ
a	aa	i	ee	u	oo	Ru

એ	ઐ	ઓ	ઔ	અં	અઃ
e	ai	o	ou	aM	aha

ક	ખ	ગ	ઘ	ઙ
ka	kha	ga	gha	nga

ચ	છ	જ	ઝ	ઞ
cha	chha	ja	jha	nya

ટ	ઠ	ડ	ઢ	ણ
Ta	Tha	Da	Dha	Na

ત	થ	દ	ધ	ન
ta	tha	da	dha	na

પ	ફ	બ	ભ	મ
pa	pha	ba	bha	ma

ય	ર	લ	વ	શ	ષ
ya	ra	la	va	sha	Sha

સ	હ	ળ	ક્ષ	જ્ઞ
sa	ha	La	kSha	gnya

Let's begin with the consonants.

The Gujarati consonants are grouped in rows according to the parts of the mouth used to pronounce them. The consonants form the basic building blocks, so once you have mastered these, you will be well on your way to reading and writing this beautiful language!

ક

ક *is for* કાચબો.
(ka)   (kaachbo)

He walks kind of slow.

But in a race with સસલું,
                    (sasluM)

પહેલું કોણ આવ્યું?
(paheluM   koN   aavyuM?)

ખ _is for_ ખેતી.
(kha)　　　　(khetee)

Fruits and vegetables – nature's display;

રીંગણ કે ભીંડા – શું ખાશો તમે?
(reengaN　ke　bheenDaa)　　(shuM　khaasho　tame?)

ગ   ઘ

ગ *is for* ગરબા.
(ga)   (garbaa)

We dance for નવરાત્રી's nine nights.
(navraatree's)

ઘડિયાળમાં બાર વાગ્યા!
(ghaDiyaaLmaaM   baar   vaagyaa!)

Time to turn off the lights.

ચ

ચ *is for* ચકલી.
(cha)   (chaklee)

She comes to my door .

એને દાણા ચણવા છે?
(ene   daaNaa   chaNvaa   chhe?)

I think she wants some more.

છ

છ *is for* છત્રી.
(ccha)   (cchatree)

વરસાદ પડે છે!
(varsaad   paDe chhe!)

The monsoon clouds look magical –
A billowy, gray miracle.

જ is for જલેબી.
(ja)　　　　　(jalebee)

I wish they grew on a ઝાડ.
(jhaaD)

Like a ફૂલ or a ફળ –
(phool)　　　(phaL)

Although, that would be quite odd.

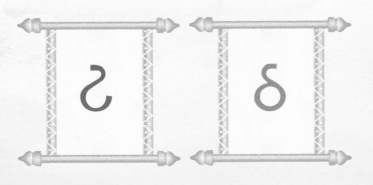

ટ *is for* ટોપી.
(Ta)　　　　(Topee)

It can keep the sun rays away.

ઠંડીમાં પણ જોઇએ!
(ThanDee-maaM paN　joiye!)

Which one do I need today?

S _is for_ સબો .
(Da)   (Dabbo)

I wonder what's inside.

ખોલીને તું જોઈ લે...
(kholeene   tuM   jo-ee   le)

What yummy treats it hides.

ઢ ણ

ઢ *is for* ઢોલ.
(Dh)   (Dhol)

દૂરથી અવાજ સંભળાય.
(doorthee   avaaj   sambhaLaay.)

There must be a wedding –

Can you hear the શરણાઈ?
(sharNaai)

ત

ત *is for* તબલાં.
(ta)   (tablaaM)

It helps to keep the beat —

While દીદી plays the સિતાર:
(deedee)   (sitaar)

એક – બે – ત્રણ – ચાર!
(ek   – be – traN – chaar!)

થ *is for* થાળી.
(tha)   (thaaLee)

I have one made of steel.

દાળ, ભાત, શાક, રોટલી આપો!
(daaL,   bhaat,   shaak,   roTlee   aapo!)

Now it's time for a meal!

ૐ *is for* દિવાળી –
(da) (divaaLee)

A season for our New Year.

ફટાકડા, દીવા, અને રંગોળી –
(faTaakaDaa, deevaa, ane rangoLee)

Create a festive atmosphere.

ધ *is for* ધ્વજ.
(dha)   (dhvaj)

We salute it each day.

Waving high in the sky —

"વંદે માતરમ!" અમે ગાઈએ.
("vande maataram!")   ame   gaa-ee-e.)

ન

ન *is for* નદી.
(na)   (nadee)

Peacefully the ગંગા flows.
(gangaa)

From the હિમાલય પર્વતમાળા –
(himaalay   parvatmaaLaa)

Into the દરિયો it goes.
(dariyo)

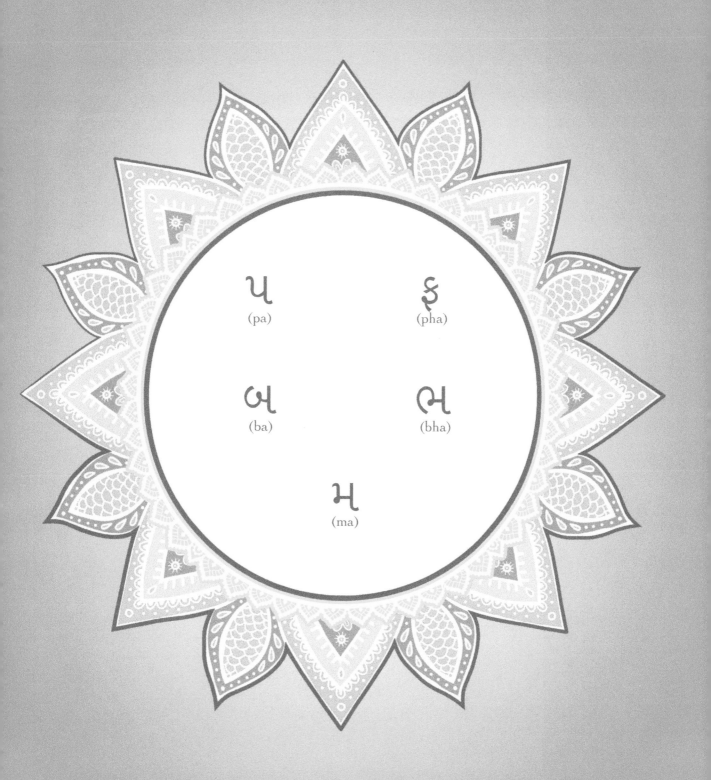

પ is for પતંગ.
(pa)   (patang)

On ઉત્તરાયણ they fill the sky.
(uttaraayaN)

"કાઈપો છે!" હું જોરથી બોલું.
("kaipo   chhe!" huM jorthee boluM.)

"Now પપ્પા, can I try?"
(pappaa)

ફ

ફ *is for* ફળ .
(pha)   (phaL)

My mummy packs them for lunch.

સફરજન, કેરી, અને કેળું –
(sapharjan,   keree,   ane   keLuM)

But if it's દ્રાક્ષ, I'll eat a bunch!
(draakSh)

બ *is for* બંસી .
(ba)　　　　　(bansee)

શ્રી કૃષ્ણ's was made of bamboo.
(shree kriShNa's)

ભગવાન played music so divine,
(bhagvaan)

We sing His ભજન in our shrine.
(bhajan)

મ is for માછલી.
(ma)   (maachhlee)

મત્સ્ય અવતાર was the first.
(matsya   avataar)

The tiny fish grew, you know?

Then Manu realized –

"તમે ભગવાન વિષ્ણુ છો!"
("tame   bhagvaan   viShNu   chho!")

ય (ya)   ર (ra)   લ (la)   વ (va)

શ (sha)   ષ (Sha)   સ (sa)   હ (ha)

ળ (La)   ક્ષ (kSha)   જ્ઞ (gnya)

ય *is for* **યોગ.**
(ya)   (yoga)

સૂર્ય નમસ્કાર helps my health.
(soorya   namaskaar)

શરીર અને મન મજબૂત બનાવે છે –
(shareer   ane   man   majboot   banaave   chhe)

That is life's true wealth!

ર *is for* **રિક્ષા** –
(ra)   (rikShaa)
I take it to the station.
ટ્રેનમાં બેસીને સૂરત જાઇએ –
(train-maM   beseene   soorat   jaiye)
For our family vacation.

લ

લ _is for_ લાકડી.
(la)   (laakDee)

ગાંધીજી used one to help him walk.
(gandheejee)

With અહિંસા and સત્ય he fought,
(ahimsaa)   (satya)

To give the British Empire a shock.

વ *is for* વાલ્મિકી .
(va)   (vaalmikee)

He wrote the રામાયણ.
(raamaayaN)

રામ, સીતા, હનુમાન, લક્ષ્મણ –
(raam,   seetaa,   hanumaan,   lakShman)

They won my heart, one by one.

ષ

ષ *is for* ષટ્કોણ –
(Sha)   (ShaTkoN)

A shape with six sides.

ત્રિકોણ કે ચોરસ – શું દોરું ?
(trikoN   ke   choras   – shuM doruM?)

Oh, I must decide.

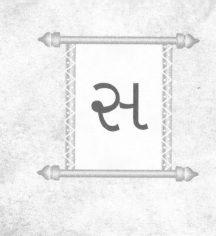

સ *is for* સાડી .
(sa) (saaDee)

We are going to the wedding.

કેટલા વાગ્યા? જલદી કરો!
(keTlaa vaagyaa? jaldee karo!)

Everybody is waiting.

હ *is for* હોળી .
(ha)   (hoLee)

There is color in the air:

લાલ, પીળો, ભૂરો, અને લીલો –
(laal,   peeLo,   bhooro,   ane   leelo)

Let's wash it out of my hair!

ળ ક્ષ જ્ઞ

ળ, ક્ષ, *and* જ્ઞ .
(La) (kSha) (gna)

They are the final consonants.

પતી ગયું? વધારે આપો!
(patee gayuM? vadhaare aapo!)

Let's go on to the vowels at once!

Now that we've learned our consonants, let's bring them to life with our vowels.

The Gujarati vowels are grouped in pairs of short and long sounds. Unlike the consonants, which are typically written out separately, you will most commonly find the vowels combined with a consonant using "*maatras.*" After you learn the vowels individually, see if you can identify the *maatra* that represents each vowel!

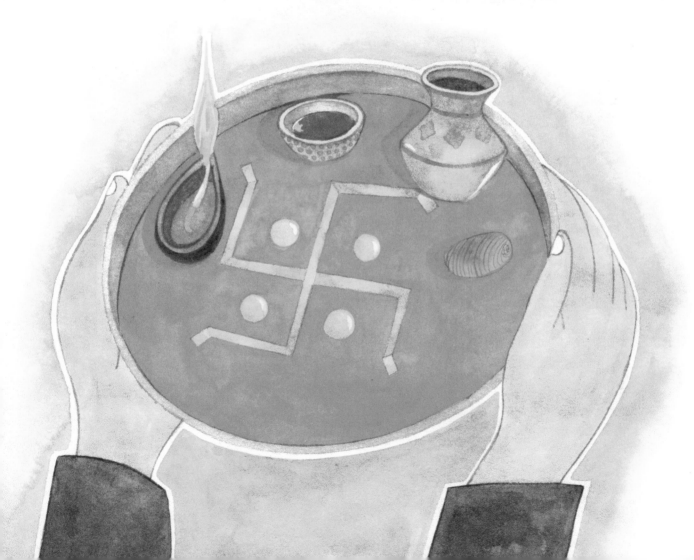

અ *is for* અગ્નિ .
(a)   (agni)

We light the આરતીનો દીવો.
(aarateeno   deevo)

We ask God to bless us –
જગમાં કાયમ અમન રહો.
(jagamaaM   kaayam   aman   raho.)

ઈ *is for* ઈડલી –
(i)   (iDlee)

A dish from the દક્ષિણ.
                (dakShiN)

ઉત્તરમાં છે પંજાબ.
(uttarmaaM chhe panjaab.)

What do they eat in પૂર્વ અને પશ્ચિમ?
           (poorva ane   paSchim)

ઈ *is for* ઇંટ .
(ee)   (eenT)

બનાવો મોટું ઘર.
(banaavo   moTuM   ghar)

Built it carefully.

મને તો પડવાનો ડર!
(mane   to   paDvaano   Dar!)

ઉ *is for* ઉંદર –
(u) (undar)

Running through my ઘર.
(ghar)

I don't have any ઉન for you.
(oon)

What else can you chew?

ઋ *is for* ઋતુ .
(Ru)   (Rutu)

In વસંત the flowers bloom;
(vasant)

ઉનાળો brings a lot of heat;
(unaaLo)

And શિયાળો some gloom.
(shiyaaLo)

એ _is for_ એક –
(e)　　　　(ek)
Rare, singular, and unique.

Like ઐરાવત – Lord Indra's વાહન,
(airaavat)　　　　　　(vaahan)
Who was born from a milky ocean.

ઓ *is for* ઓશીકું.
(o)　　　　　(osheekuM)
I lay down on it to rest.
"Just a spoonful, please don't quibble."

"Mummy, this ઔષધ is terrible!"
(ouShadh)

અં   અઃ

અં *is for* અંધારું.
(aM)   (andhaaruM)
I can't sleep, it's so bright.

અઃ! There is the switch —
(aha)
Turn it off and say good night!

Glossary

In order of appearance:

Gujarati	Pronunciation	English
કેમ છો?	/ke-m chho/	How are you?
મજામાં છો?	/ma-jaa-maaM chho/	Are you well?
મારું નામ કવિ છે.	/maa-ruM naa-m ka-vi chhe/	My name is Kavi.
ગુજરતી શીખવા તૈયાર છો?	/gu-ja-raa-tee shee-kh-vaa tai-yaa-r chho/	Are you ready to learn Gujarati?
કાચબો	/kaa-ch-bo/	A tortoise.
સસલું	/sa-s-luM/	A rabbit (hare).
પહેલું કોણ આવ્યું?	/pa-he-luM ko-N aa-vyuM/	Who came first?
ખેતી	/khe-tee/	A farm.
રીંગણ કે ભીંડા – શું ખાશો તમે?	/reen-ga-N ke bheen-Daa/ -/shu khaa-sho ta-me/	Eggplant or Okra – What will you eat?
ગરબા	/ga-r-baa/	A traditional folk dance from Gujarat popular during the Navratri festival.
નવરાત્રી	/na-v-raa-tree/	A Hindu festival celebrated over nine nights and ten days during September/October honoring womanhood and Goddess Durga.
ઘડિયાળમાં બાર વાગ્યા!	/gha-Di-yaa-L-maaM baa-r vaa-gyaa/	The clock struck 12.
ચકલી	/cha-k-lee/	A sparrow.
એને દાણા ચણવા છે?	/e-ne daa-Naa chaa-N-vaa chhe/	Does she want to eat seeds?
છત્રી	/ccha-tree/	An umbrella.
વરસાદ પડે છે!	/va-r-saa-d pa-De chhe/	It is raining!
જલેબી	/ja-le-bee/	An Indian sweet made by deep-frying wheat flour batter in coiled, circular shapes, which are then soaked in sugar syrup.
ઝાડ	/jhaa-D/	A tree.
ફૂલ	/phoo-l/	A flower.
ફળ	/pha-L/	Fruit.
ટોપી	/To-pee/	A hat.
ઠંડીમાં પણ જોઈએ!	/Than-Dee-maaM pa-N jo-i-e/	You also need it when it is cold!
ડબ્બો	/Da-bbo/	A container.
ખોલીને તું જોઈ લે...	/kho-lee-ne tuM jo-ee le/	Open it and see…
ઢોલ	/Dho-l/	A large elongated, double-headed drum.
દૂરથી અવાજ સંભળાય.	/doo-r-thee a-vaa-j sam-bha-Laa-y/	You can hear the noise from afar.
શરણાઈ	/sha-r-Naa-i/	An ancient double-reeded woodwind instrument.
તબલાં	/ta-b-laaM/	A pair of small hand drums fundamental to Hindustani classical music. Individually, the larger daya is played with the right hand, and the baya is played with the left hand.
દીદી	/dee-dee/	Elder sister.
સિતાર	/si-taa-r/	A large, long-necked Indian stringed instrument used mainly in Hindustani classical music.
એક – બે – ત્રણ – ચાર!	/e-k – be – tra-N – chaa-r/	Counting: 1-2-3-4.
થાળી	/thaa-Lee/	A plate.

દાળ, ભાત, શાક, રોટલી આપો!	/daa-L, bhaa-t, shaa-k, ro-T-lee aa-po/	Traditional everyday Gujarati meal consisting of lentils, rice, vegetables, and flatbread.
દિવાળી	/di-vaa-Lee/	Also called Deepavali, it is one of India's major holidays that generally falls in the months of October or November. In Gujarat, the next day after Diwali is celebrated as the Gujarati New Year.
ફટાકડા, દીવા, અને રંગોળી	/fa-Taa-ka-Daa, dee-vaa, a-ne ran-go-Lee/	Fireworks, a small oil lamp, and colored floor art.
ધ્વજ	/dhva-j/	A flag.
"વંદે માતરમ!" અમે ગાઈએ.	/"van-de maa-ta-ra-m!" a-me gaa-ee-e/	We sing, "Vande Mataram!"
નદી	/na-dee/	A river.
ગંગા	/gan-gaa/	The Ganga River (Ganges).
હિમાલય પર્વતમાળા	/hi-maa-la-y pa-rva-t-maa-Laa/	The Himalaya mountains.
દરિયો	/da-ri-yo/	An ocean.
પતંગ	/pa-tan-g/	A kite.
ઉત્તરાયણ	/u-tta-raa-ya-N/	A kite-flying festival celebrated grandly in Gujarat on January 14.
"કાઈપો છે!" હું જોરથી બોલું.	/"ka-i-po chhe!" hu jo-r-thee bo-luM/	I loudly say, "It [the kite] is cut!"
પપ્પા	/pa-ppa/	Dad.
ફળ	/pha-L/	Fruit.
સફરજન, કેરી, અને કેળું	/sa-pha-r-ja-n, ke-ree, ane ke-LuM/	Apple, mango, and banana
દ્રાક્ષ	/draa-kSh/	Grapes.
બંસી	/ban-see/	A flute.
શ્રીકૃષ્ણ	/shree kRu-ShNa/	Lord Vishnu's eighth avatar
ભગવાન	/bha-g-vaa-n/	God.
ભજન	/bha-ja-n/	A devotional hymn or song.
માછલી	/maa-chh-lee/	A fish.
મત્સ્ય અવતાર	/ma-tsya a-va-taa-r/	According to Hindu Mythology, the first incarnation of Lord Vishnu is in the form of a fish, known as Matsya.
"તમે ભગવાન વિષ્ણુ છો!"	/"ta-me bha-ga-vaa-n vi-ShNu chho!"/	"You are Lord Vishnu!"
યોગ	/yo-ga/	Yoga. A Hindu spiritual discipline prescribing a system of exercises for mental and physical health.
સૂર્ય નમસ્કાર	/soo-rya na-ma-skaa-r/	Sun Salutation, comprising a sequence of 12 asanas.
શરીર અને મન મજબૂત બનાવે છે	/sha-ree-r a-ne ma-n ma-j-boo-t ba-naa-ve chhe/	Make my body and mind strong.
રિક્ષા	/ri-kShaa/	A three-wheeled passenger cart with a covered seat for passengers behind the driver.
ટ્રેનમાં બેસીને સૂરત જાઈએ	/Tre-n-maaM be-see-ne soo-ra-t jaa-i-e/	We sit in a train and go to Surat (a city in Gujarat).
લાકડી	/laa-k-Dee/	A wooden stick.
ગાંધીજી	/gaan-dhee-jee/	Mohandas Karamchand (Mahatma) Gandhi.
અહિંસા	/a-him-saa/	The principle of non-violence toward all living things.

સત્ય	/sa-tya/	Truth.
વાલ્મિકી	/vaal-mi-kee/	An Indian sage who is credited with writing the epic Ramayana.
રામાયણ	/raa-maa-ya-N/	A Sanskrit epic narrating the life of Lord Rama – Lord Vishnu's seventh avatar. It is one of the largest ancient epics in world literature.
રામ, સીતા, હનુમાન, લક્ષ્મણ	/raa-m, see-taa, ha-numaa-n, la-kShma-N/	The principle characters in The Ramayana.
ષટ્કોણ	/Sha-T-ko-N/	A hexagon.
ત્રિકોણ કે ચોરસ – શું દોરું?	/tri-ko-N ke cho-ra-s – shuM do-ruM/	Triangle or square – What should I draw?
સાડી	/saa-Dee/	A traditional garment worn by women in India.
કેટલા વાગ્યા? જલદી કરો!	/ke-T-laa vaa-gyaa? ja-l-dee ka-ro!/	What time is it? Hurry up!
હોળી	/ho-Lee/	A Hindu spring festival that usually falls in the month of March. It is known as the "Festival of Colors."
લાલ, પીળો, ભૂરો, અને લીલો.	/laa-l, pee-Lo, bhoo-ro, a-ne lee-lo/	Red, yellow, blue, and green.
પતી ગયું? વધારે આપો!	/pa-tee ga-yuM? va-dhaa-re aa-po!/	Is it over? Give me more!
અગ્નિ	/a-gni/	A fire (also refers to the Hindu God of Fire).
આરતીનો દીવો	/aa-ra-tee-no dee-vo/	A Hindu ritual of worship in which a small flame that is placed on a plate is rotated in front of a deity.
જગમાં કાયમ અમન રહો.	/ja-ga-maaM kaa-ya-m a-ma-n ra-ho/	May peace prevail always in the world.
ઈડલી	/i-D-lee/	A small, round South Indian steamed cake made of rice and lentils.
દક્ષિણ	/da-kShi-N/	South.
ઉત્તરમાં છે પંજાબ.	/u-tta-r-maaM chhe pan-jaa-b/	There is Punjab in the North.
પૂર્વ	/poo-rva/	East.
પશ્ચિમ	/pa-Schi-m/	West.
ઈંટ	/een-T/	A brick.
બનાવો મોટું ઘર.	/ba-naa-vo mo-TuM gha-r/	Make a big house.
મને તો પડવાનો ડર!	/ma-ne to pa-Da-vaa-no Dar/	I am afraid of it falling!
ઉંદર	/un-da-r/	A mouse.
ઘર	/gha-r/	A house.
ઊન	/oo-n/	Wool.
ઋતુ	/Ru-tu/	Season.
વસંત	/va-san-t/	Spring.
ઉનાળો	/u-naa-Lo/	Summer.
શિયાળો	/shi-yaa-Lo/	Winter.
એક	/e-k/	The number one.
ઐરાવત	/ai-raa-va-t/	A mythological white elephant who carries the Hindu god Indra.
વાહન	/vaa-ha-n/	A Sanskrit term for vehicle.
ઓશીકું	/o-shee-kuM/	A pillow.
ઔષધ	/ou-Sha-dh/	Medicine.
અંધારું	/an-dhaa-ruM/	Darkness.

ચાલો ગુજરાતી બોલીએ!
(chaalo gujaraatee boleeye!)

Let's talk in Gujarati!

તું કેમ છે?/તમે કેમ છો?
(tuM kem chhe?) (tame kem chho?)

How are you? (Informal) / How are you? (Formal)

હું મજામાં છું.
(huM majaamaaM chhuM.)

I am doing well.

તારું નામ શું છે? / તમારું નામ શું છે?
(taaruM naam shuM chhe?) (tamaaruM naam shuM chhe?)

What is your name? (Informal) / What is your name (Formal).

મારું નામ _____ છે.
(maaruM naam _____ chhe.)

My name is _____.

તું ક્યાં રહે છે?/ તમે ક્યાં રહો છો?
(tuM kyaaM rahe chhe?) (tame kyaaM raho chho?)

Where do you live? (Informal) / Where do you live? (Formal).

હું ____ માં રહું છું.
(huM _____ maaM rahuM chhuM.)

I live in _____.

તું કેટલા વર્ષની છે?
tuM keTlaa varSh-nee chhe?

How old are you? (said to female)

તું કેટલા વર્ષનો છે?
tuM keTlaa varSh-no chhe?

How old are you? (said to male)

હું _____ વર્ષની છું.
huM ____ varSh-nee chhuM.

I am ____ years old. (said by female).

હું _____ વર્ષનો છું.
huM ____ varSh-no chhuM.

I am ____ years old. (said by male)

Gujarati Cardinals:			Gujarati Ordinals:			Gujarati Colors:		
1	એક	/e-k/	1st	પહેલું	/pa-he-luM/	Red	લાલ	/laa-l/
2	બે	/be/	2nd	બીજું	/bee-juM/	Orange	નારંગી	/naa-ran-gee/
3	ત્રણ	/tra-N/	3rd	ત્રીજું	/tree-juM/	Yellow	પીળો	/pee-Lo/
4	ચાર	/chaa-r/	4th	ચોથું	/cho-thuM/	Green	લીલો	/lee-lo/
5	પાંચ	/paan-ch/	5th	પાંચમું	/paan-ch-muM/	Blue	ભૂરો	/bhoo-ro/
6	છ	/chha/	6th	છઠ્ઠું	/chha-TTuM/	Purple	જંબલી	/jaam-ba-lee/
7	સાત	/saa-t/	7th	સાતમું	/saa-t-muM/	Pink	ગુલાબી	/gu-laa-bee/
8	આઠ	/aa-Th/	8th	આઠમું	/aa-Th-muM/	Black	કાળો	/kaa-Lo/
9	નવ	/na-v/	9th	નવમું	/na-v-muM/	White	સફેદ	/sa-phe-d/
10	દસ	/da-s/	10th	દસમું	/da-s-muM/	Brown	રાખોડી	/raa-kho-Dee/

તું શાળામાં જાય છે?	Do you go to school?
tuM shaaLaa-maaM jaay chhe?	
હા, હું શાળામાં જાઉં છું.	Yes, I go to school.
haa, huM shaaLaa-maaM jaa-uM chhuM.	
તું કયા ધોરણમાં છે?	Which grade are you in?
tuM kayaa dhoraN-maaM chhe?	
હું _____ ધોરણમાં છું.	I am in _____ grade.
hooM _____ dhoraN-maaM chhuM.	
મારે એક બહેન છે. એ મારા કરતાં નાની છે.	I have one sister. She is younger than me.
maare ek ben chhe. e maaraa kartaaM naanee chhe.	
તને ભાઈ કે બહેન છે?	Do you have any brothers or sisters?
tane bhaa-ee ke ben chhe?	
હા, મારે _____ ભાઈ (ભાઈઓ) છે.	Yes, I have _____ brother(s).
haa, maare _____ bhaa-ee (baa-eeyo) chhe.	
હા, મારે _____ બહેન (બહેનો) છે.	Yes, I have _____ sister(s).
haa, maare _____ ben chhe.	
મારે દાળ, ભાત, શાક, રોટલી ખાવાં છે.	I want to eat daal-bhaat-shaak-rotli.
maare daaL, bhaat, shaak, roTlee khaavaaM chhe.	
તારે શું ખાવું છે?	What do you want to eat?
taare shuM khaavuM chhe?	
મારે _____ ખાવું છે.	I want to eat _____.
maare _____ khaavuM chhe.	
મને લીલો રંગ ગમે છે.	I like the color green.
mane leelo rang game chhe.	
તને કેવો રંગ ગમે?	What color do you like?
tane kevo rang game?	
મને _____ રંગ ગમે છે.	I like the color _____.
mane _____ rang game chhe.	
તારે શું રમવું છે?	What do you want to play?
taare shuM ramvuM chhe?	
મારે _____ રમવું છે.	I want to play _____.
maare _____ ramvuM chhe.	
આવજો!	Goodbye!
aavjo!	

Lightning Source UK Ltd.
Milton Keynes UK
UKHW051257161222
413868UK00010B/147